CW01072273

# CELEBRITIES' FAVOURITE BOOKS

# CELEBRITIES' FAVOURITE BOOKS

Compiled by Jeff Thorburn

Foreword by Princess Alexandra

APEX PUBLISHING LTD

Hardback first published in 2009 by

# Apex Publishing Ltd

PO Box 7086, Clacton on Sea, Essex, CO15 5WN, England

**www.apexpublishing.co.uk**

Copyright © 2009 by Jeff Thorburn
The author has asserted his moral rights

**British Library Cataloguing-in-Publication Data**
**A catalogue record for this book**
**is available from the British Library**

ISBN 978-1-906358-63-1           1-906358-63-X

All rights reserved. This book is sold subject to the condition that no part of this book is to be reproduced, in any shape or form. Or by way of trade, stored in a retrieval system or transmitted in any form or by any means, electronic, mechanical, photocopying, recording, be lent, re-sold, hired out or otherwise circulated in any form of binding or cover other than that in which it is published and without a similar condition, including this condition being imposed on the subsequent purchaser, without prior permission of the copyright holder.

Typeset in 12pt Times New Roman

Production Manager: Chris Cowlin

Cover Design: Siobhan Smith

Printed by the MPG Books Group in the UK

*This book is dedicated with love to Evelyn Doughty and in loving memory of Bert Doughty who sacrificed his own health caring for her.*

*This book is also for all those who suffer from dementia and all those who are dedicated to their care.*

# ACKNOWLEDGEMENTS

I would like to thank all those who were generous and sympathetic enough to share their private thoughts and contribute to this book. Without them this fundraising effort would not be possible.

I would also like to thank Chris Cowlin at Apex Publishing Ltd for agreeing to take on this project with such enthusiasm.

Thanks also to John Morris for suggesting the idea for the project.

Finally I would like to thank you, the reader, for buying this book and thus contributing to the work of the Alzheimer's Society. I hope you get as much enjoyment from these pages as I did when I received the letters and prepared the manuscript.

*Jeff Thorburn*

# FOREWORD

This book is dedicated to Evelyn Doughty, who has been living with vascular dementia for several years.

Her son-in-law Jeff Thorburn, hopes the book will raise much needed funds for the Alzheimer's Society.

This book is destined to achieve enduring appeal and I hope you will enjoy reading it.

*Princess Alexandra*

# INTRODUCTION

After watching my mother-in-law, Evelyn, suffer from dementia for several years and seeing the effect this has had on both her as a person and the family, I felt compelled to try to raise funds for the Alzheimer's Society in the hope that further research can help to understand this terrible affliction and maybe even find a cure.

The Alzheimer's Society does great work in raising awareness of the issues surrounding dementia in all its forms, and helps both sufferers and carers with advice and information and provides practical support. It also researches the causes, nature and treatment of dementia.

In order to raise funds, I decided to write to famous people, asking them to explain what their favourite book is and why. I felt that by asking people to express their appreciation of their favourite book this would hopefully encourage others to read novels they may never have considered. At the same time, it would be a good way of raising funds for the Alzheimer's Society and raising awareness of the work it does and the plight of those who suffer from dementia.

The responses I received are contained within this book. Many who contributed confided that dementia had also affected their family in some way and hoped the book would succeed in raising funds for such a worthy cause.

# BRIAN ALDISS
## *WRITER/CRITIC*

It is difficult to choose an entirely favourite book. Over the space of a long lifetime there are several I would once have named. For instance, as a young boy, I would probably have named **THE WORLD IN DARKNESS** by Murray Roberts, an adventure featuring Captain Justice, my boyhood hero!

Later on, there are several of Thomas Hardy's novels, most notably **THE MAYOR OF CASTERBRIDGE**, but also his beautiful smaller novels, such as **THE WOODLANDERS**, the inescapable choice of Jane Austen's **PRIDE AND PREJUDICE** and some of Charles Dickens' novels - **GREAT EXPECTATIONS** in particular. Rather less obviously, I would name **THE LOST STEPS** by the Cuban-born writer Alejo Carpentier, which my wife and I have read time and time again.

But my favourite novel of later years is not one of these illustrious titles. For me, the most cherished novel is Leo Tolstoy's most neglected novel **RESURRECTION**. I have three translations of this novel on my shelves, of which the one I most prefer is the translation made by Rosemary Edmonds, published by Penguin Books.

This is the novel the mighty Tolstoy wrote in 1899, in his old age. He died in 1910, at a time when a camera was present to record the masses who attended his passing and to pay him homage.

**RESURRECTION** provides us with a panorama not only of Russia, but of humanity in general; it depicts something of the aristocratic life as rendered in **ANNA KARENINA**, while also giving a vivid picture of the underworld.

The chief character in the book is Count Nekhlyudov. Nekhlyudov in his aristocratic youth has wronged a woman, by name Maslova, who was in his employ. Many years later he finds himself acting as judge over a small number of criminals, among whom Maslova is a defendant. Maslova, although still beautiful, has been hardened by her experiences among the lower orders of society into whose company she has been plunged. It is Nekhlyudov's decision to make up for the wrong he did the young woman. When he asks her to forgive him, that is something she cannot and will not do. So this great story continues with the Count eventually deciding that he must marry Maslova. He follows Maslova into exile in Siberia.

Among the many difficult questions Tolstoy asks is this one in Chapter 30: "Why and by what right does one class of people lock up, torture, exile, flog and kill other people, when they themselves are no better than those whom they torture, flog and kill?"

The whole theme of the book concerns the importance of repentance and forgiveness. I find it profound and salutary for us today, when so many films from Hollywood - to take an instance - seem to glorify Revenge, the destructive opposite of Forgiveness.
The more I re-read this, Tolstoy's last novel, the more I am struck by its grandeur and by the many characters who inhabit it. Also, I have deep sympathy for the concluding paragraph of the novel, which runs as follows:

2

"That night an entirely new life began for Nekhlyudov, not so much because he had entered into new conditions of life but because everything that happened to him from that time on was endowed with an entirely different meaning for him. How this new chapter of his life will end, the future will show."

My own experience convinces me that Tolstoy is as penetratingly truthful here as in the rest of his book.

# MOHAMMED AL FAYED

## *OWNER OF HARRODS*

My favourite book is **BRING HOME THE REVOLUTION** (How Britain can live the American dream) by Jonathan Freedland.

I am very taken by this book (published in 1998 by Fourth Estate) because it echoes my own view of what is wrong with the way Britain is governed and sets out in a clear and amusing way why things have gone wrong and what it is about the American way of life and political system that the British would do well to adopt.

Freedland looks at the way the British have imported American culture and decides that we are not getting the best of it - it is richer than we ever imagined. I conclude that the dreams of many of today's British reformers have already been made real in the United States. The American ideal is actually our own. Contrary to received wisdom, Britain did have a revolution - but we had it in America. Now is the time for British republicanism.

# JEFFREY ARCHER
## *WRITER*

I'm afraid it is impossible for me to name just one favourite book, so here is a list of my all-time favourites:

**DISRAELI** by Robert Blake
Disraeli is for me a political hero, and this particular biography is written with such style and academic muscle that I remain in awe of the author.

**THE DIAMOND AS BIG AS THE RITZ** by F Scott Fitzgerald
A wonderful set of short stories; whimsically written by a great storyteller and, what's more, when you have finished with them, you can turn to **BERNICE BOBS HER HAIR.**

**REUNION** by Fred Uhlman
As a gentile, this short book gave me an insight into the problems of being a Je wish child in 1930s Germany, which I find much more poignant than many long films on the holocaust.

**NELSON** by Christopher Hibbert
My biggest hero - warts and all; this award-winning biography is also a page-turner. I also came to have an understanding and sympathy for his mistress.

**DUVEEN** by S N Behrman
This is the story of the amazing art collector and dealer, Joseph Duveen, and his association with Bernard Berenson; were they a couple of crooks, or just good

businessmen?

**THE THIRTY-NINE STEPS** by John Buchan
Still the master at telling a simple story, so it's
"unputdownable"; the sort of book that even snobby
critics have to admit is a good read.

# JANE ASHER
## *ACTRESS*

My favourite book is **THE BLACK PRI NCE** by Iris Murdoch. She has to be one of my favourite writers in any case, and this particular novel was written at a time when she was at the height of her powers. (Having just written that sentence, I am amazed to realise that I have picked someone who – famously – developed Alzheimer's later in her life. The fact that I chose this particular author, and that this book is raising funds for the Alzheimer's Society, is sheer coincidence: I chose her and the novel purely from my personal love for her work).

Iris Murdoch was, of course, a brilliant philosopher, and she always slipped some wonderfully philosophical observations into her writing. Later in her career she took this much further, and I always suspected that the early and mid-career novels were only part of a semi-planned progression towards her real purpose – to teach us all the complexities of philosophical thought.

**THE BLACK PRINCE** was written at a time when she was at her most accessible and entertaining, and the gloriously cynical humour and brilliantly observed and described range of human behaviour is a joy to read. It also contains one of the best ever descriptions of the moment of falling (or the realisation that you have already fallen!) in love.

# EILEEN ATKINS
## *ACTRESS/WRITER*

I have so many favourite books that it's really impossible to choose. When I was about eight, my favourite book was **THE WIND IN THE WILLOWS** by Kenneth Grahame. Then in my teens it was **ANNA KARENINA**, Tolstoy's great love story. In my thirties I was mad about Ford Maddox Ford's **THE GOOD SOLDIER** subtitled **A TALE OF PASSION** and in between and since, I have of course adored every book of Jane Austen's and most of Charles Dickens' - my favourites of his being **GREAT EXPECTATIONS** and **DAVID COPPERFIELD.**

There are many modern writers I like as well: William Boyd; Elizabeth Jane Howard (particularly **THE CAZALET QUARTET**); and Joanna Trollope and Philip Roth to name but a few. But if I had to choose one book, then it would have to be by Virginia Woolf; not one of her novels, although I think both **TO THE LIGHTHOUSE** and **MRS DALLOWAY** are sheer magic, but her diaries which can be bought in a shortened form (there are actually many volumes), edited by Olivier Bell, called **A MOMENT'S LIBERTY**. What you get are the day-to-day thoughts of a witty, wildly imaginative, extremely funny, clever, immensely curious observer of life. You will never think again, 'Oh, Virginia Woolf, wasn't she the one who went mad and put stones in her pockets and drowned herself?' Well, yes she did do that when she was fifty-nine, but she's not remotely depressing to read; she's huge fun and illuminates one's own view of life.

You can dip in and out of the book as well, so on a dreary day you can say to yourself, 'I think I'll just read a few pages of Virginia.' I swear to God you'll put the book down feeling much better.

# PAM AYRES
## *WRITER/POET*

One of my favourite books is **FRIED GREEN TOMATOES AT THE WHISTLE STOP CAFÉ** by Fannie Flagg. It's a smashing read, touching, funny and a bit horrifying too. I really felt as if I was there.

# GEORGE BAKER
## *ACTOR/WRITER/DIRECTOR*

I have many, many favourite books, but one that I often read and, for obvious reasons, is near to me, is **I CLAUDIUS**. Some reasons why I think it is so readable are, that firstly Robert Graves is a wonderful storyteller. Secondly, he is an immaculate historian. Thirdly, but in a way the best of all is that he writes with such humour and delight in his subject and, of course, the characters, which you would think were fictitious as they are so larger than life. That is, of course, until you look closely into the American political scene and even perhaps into ours. Sleaze, corruption, power-seeking, murder and mayhem are still with us. Oh yes, **I CLAUDIUS** is a very modern novel.

# JOAN BAKEWELL
## *BROADCASTER/WRITER*

My favourite book is **ONE HUNDRED YEARS OF SOLITUDE** by Gabriel Marquez. I like its long family story and the strange unfolding of the family history, told with such imaginative resources, a great book!

# TONY BENN
## *RETIRED POLITICIAN*

**THE GUINNESS BOOK OF RECORDS** would be my choice. It shows us how much each of us can achieve.

# DR PAT BIDMEAD
*POET/SOCIAL PSYCHOLOGIST*

**THE OUTSIDER** by Albert Camus

My first introduction to **THE OUTSIDER** was through a French friend when I was in my early twenties and it left a lasting impression on me. The impact was immediate and influenced my thinking. A second reading added to my understanding and continues to influence me in even more profound ways.

In those early years of my life, I considered myself very much an outsider and therefore, could identify very easily with Camus' character Meursault if only in a superficial way that benefited me and gave justification to my more immature beliefs. I did not hold conventional positions on most of the practices or ideas circulating in my time. I had no hang-ups about my denial of nationalism or a monarchy I did not believe in and little time for those who believed differently about such matters. I was a republican born and bred in Windsor where such a stance was almost unheard of at that time. No way did I feel I fitted into the social norms of my time or community.

**THE OUTSIDER** reinforced my beliefs and made me even more determined to practise them, protesting about all the things that I could not go along with and still able to maintain an easy conscience. I was an individual rebelling against being socialised into norms of my culture in which I had no belief. I could not, and I would not, play hypocritical games.

The deeper psychological and spiritual dimensions of the book did not sink in until some years later to give me a deeper, more realistic understanding of myself. At the superficial level, the main character will not lie to satisfy the feelings of others. He feels no emotion at the death of his mother and that is it. Later, when he is tried for murder, he refuses to admit to any regret. Through the dialogue with the lawyer, Camus conveys to the reader that in the eyes of society the innocence or guilt of Meursault relies more on not crying at his mother's funeral than on the murder he has committed. Throughout the narrative, Camus keeps returning to the theme of mother, suggesting that not all is what it seems. If Meursault really feels nothing, why does the author keep referring to her throughout the novel?

Meursault is relying, for truth, on his intellect and his emotions, but the question is one of reliability - are intellect and emotion sufficient evidence for absolute truth? His lack of emotion at his mother's death could have been a case of self-denial in order to protect himself from the deep pain of bereavement, possibly coupled with unconscious guilt feelings for putting her in a residential home, whether this action was justified or not by the circumstances. The earlier accusation made by the lawyer concerning Meursault's lack of outward grief when his mother died suggests to the reader that perhaps the lack of regret now for this murder is merely a subconscious necessity to protect his original belief that he had indeed felt no emotion at the time of his mother's death. To keep his integrity, even if based upon a misconception, he claims he will not lie to satisfy anyone.

The story spoke volumes to me and acted as a warning. Meursault has failed to grasp the fact that he, like every other human being, is body, mind and spirit, and the three interact with one another. There is also an element of arrogance - how can a mere human being ever really know absolute truth? Our intellect and emotions can help us to distinguish truth, but they are not completely accurate or reliable and when they are out of key with the spirit, which knows of a more substantial truth, there is a likelihood of conflict. We often punish ourselves for what we believe to be absolute truth.

**THE OUTSIDER** influenced me and still does in the way I interrelate with other people, never basing my judgements upon what is apparent to the eye, common sense, or my knowledge of psychology. My approach is to try to look beneath the surface of behaviour with the realisation that I can never hope to know the absolute truth about anyone, any condition, or anything in the universe. That is the province of God and he will only reveal to us what we need to know when we need to know it. We are too immature to be given the whole picture concerning the nature and workings of human beings. The knowledge is too dangerous until we evolve into beings that are more spiritual.

# ROGER BLACK
## *ATHLETE/PRESENTER*

My chosen book is **THE ALCHEMIST** by Paul Coelho.

This book personally means a lot to my wife Julia and me. It is a spiritual story about listening to your heart, pursuing your dreams and trying hard to reach your goals. You may have to take a risk or two along the way, but what you learn about yourself and others throughout the journey is worth the struggle.

# TONY BLAIR
## *FORMER PRIME MINISTER*

My favourite books as a child were **KIDNAPPED** and **TREASURE ISLAND** by Robert Louis Stevenson.

My favourite adult book is Sir Walter Scott's **IVANHOE**.

# DICKIE BIRD
## RETIRED CRICKET UMPIRE

My favourite book is my autobiography. This book was a huge success when first published, and it was the best selling sports book in history. I can certainly recommend this book to anyone who is interested not only in cricket, but in other people's lives.

# JEREMY BOWEN
*FOREIGN NEWS CORRESPONDENT/PRESENTER*

I nominate **THE WIND IN THE WILLOWS** by Kenneth Grahame as my favourite book. I liked it because when I was a kid it stimulated my imagination. I still remember how scary the scene is when Mole and Ratty get lost in the Wild Wood, until they are rescued by Badger. And, of course, there's Toad, a terrible warning to everyone …!

# JO BRAND
## *COMEDIENNE/WRITER*

I always have trouble coming up with my absolute favourite book - the cop-out answer of the closet liberal I'm afraid.

However, one of my favourite books is **IN THE SPRINGTIME OF THE YEAR** by Susan Hill. It's about a woman who loses her husband in an accident and the long, painful journey from this tragic day to some sort of acceptance and recovery. What I particularly love about it too is the rural setting. I was brought up in the country and love to read about it. It's fundamentally an optimistic novel - strange choice for me as I'm a miserable old curmudgeon underneath.

# KENNETH BRANAGH
## *ACTOR/DIRECTOR*

My favourite book as a child was **THE WIND IN THE WILLOWS** by Kenneth Grahame - I loved Toad of Toad Hall and his merry antics, especially with his motor car - poop poop!

My favourite book of all time is **DAVID COPPERFIELD** by Charles Dickens.

# RICHARD BRIERS
## *ACTOR*

My favourite book would have to be Kenneth Grahame's **THE WIND IN THE WILLOWS** which I read as a child. Many years later I played Ratty at the National Theatre which I much enjoyed. In fact, it was probably my favourite part.

# RAYMOND BRIGGS
## *AUTHOR/ILLUSTRATOR*

One of my favourite novels is **BOMBER** by Len Deighton. It tells the story of a terrifying Allied bomber raid on Germany in World War II from both points of view: that of the bomber crews and the civilians on the ground.

It is very moving and powerful. Before nuclear war, it must have been the nearest thing to hell on earth.

# GORDON BROWN
## *PRIME MINISTER*

I choose the following titles:
**THE SNAIL AND THE WHALE** – Julia Donaldson
**UNBOWED** – Wangari Maathai
**DOCHERTY** - William McIlvanney
**NEW OXFORD BOOK OF EIGHTEENTH-CENTURY VERSE** – Roger Lonsdale

I enjoy reading all kinds of books including works of fiction and biographies. I do now, of course, have the additional pleasure of reading with my two young sons, which is why I chose the first of the books in the list above.

# SIR MICHAEL CAINE
## *ACTOR*

One of my favourite books is **THE MALTESE FALCON** by Samuel Dashiell Hammett. I like it because it is a slick gangster novel set in Los Angeles which I read before I'd ever been to the city.

# The Late JAMES CALLAGHAN
## *FORMER PRIME MINISTER*

As far as books are concerned, I think that my favourite book has changed from time to time as the years have gone by. When I was very young, before World War II, I enjoyed Rudyard Kipling's groups of short stories and particularly **STALKY & CO.** Later on, after the War, I read Tolstoy's **WAR AND PEACE**, among many others, and thought that this was one of the most outstanding books that I had ever read. Later still, I went back to my schooldays and I now enjoy very much Frances Turner Palgrave's **THE GOLDEN TREASURY**. Nowadays, I find that I turn to **THE BIBLE** more than to any other book. It is a wonderful source of wisdom.

# DAVID CAMERON
## *LEADER OF THE CONSERVATIVE PARTY*

My favourite book as a child was **OUR ISLAND STORY** by Henrietta Elizabeth Marshall. This is a children's history of Britain, from the time of the Romans to the death of Queen Victoria, written in a way that really captured my imagination and nurtured my interest in the history of our great nation.

My favourite book as an adult is **GOODBYE TO ALL THAT**, Robert Grave's powerful autobiography about life in the trenches on the Western front during the First World War.

# TRACEY CHILDS
## *ACTRESS*

My all-time favourite book would have to be **A TALE OF TWO CITIES** by Charles Dickens. I first read it when I was 12 and still think it is the best thriller ever written!

# ROSEMARY CONLEY CBE
## *HEALTH AND FITNESS WRITER*

One of my favourite books has to be **THE HEART OF SUCCESS** by Rob Parsons. It is a business book that will make you laugh and make you cry. I would recommend anybody in business to read it and also to buy it for all of their managers. The book is published by Hodder and Stoughton.

# KENNETH CLARKE QC
## *POLITICIAN*

I have never really decided what my favourite book of all time is and so I will merely commend to your readers the latest book which I have almost finished reading. I had bought Roy Jenkins' memoirs enti tled **LIFE AT THE CENTRE** a few years ago, but I only got round to taking it from my shelf to read after Roy's sad death. I have always enjoyed reading most of his other political histories of other people and, in particular, his lives of Asquith and Gladstone. His own autobiography is written in the same clear and accessible style. It is extremely witty at times. He is capable of being slightly self-deprecatory and admitting mistakes without indulging in false modesty. The book is a reminder of political events well within my own memory and at the same time an enlightened and personal insight into them. I always enjoyed Roy's company and conversation. Reading his book simply underlines what a very civilised and enlightened man he was.

# NICK CLEGG
## *LEADER OF THE LIBERAL DEMOCRATS*

I have several favourite books, but one I like the most is **THE LEOPARD** by Giuseppe di Lampedusa.

This is a fantastic book and is generally recognised as one of the greatest Italian novels this century. It successfully transports the mind to the landscape of Italy in the 1860's and encourages the reader to question the nature of human frailty.

# PAUL COPLEY
## *ACTOR/WRITER*

I suppose that my favourite book - and I have to say that my favourite book is quite often whatever I'm currently reading - has got to be Thomas Hardy's novel **TESS OF THE D'URBERVILLES.**

My English teacher at Penistone Grammar School was Arthur Gill, an academic who always wore his gown, an impressive and good-humoured teacher who had the knack of making you think he was speaking only to you when he was giving forth in the classroom. When, to everybody's surprise including my own, I won the Spoken English Prize in the summer of 1959, I asked Mr Gill to suggest a novel - you could request your own prize so long as it fulfilled certain criteria - and he introduced me to the work of Thomas Hardy. I chose "Tess" primarily because much of it takes place in the countryside, in cowsheds and dairies. I grew up next to a dairy farm in West Yorkshire - I knew all the dairy herd by name and, along with my two sisters, helped with the milking and the mucking-out daily.

Like the Durbeyfields, I had ambitions (although at that time mine were in the direction of owning and riding fast motorbikes) and like Tess, most of my friends and acquaintances had something to do with the land and farming. In short, I was at the age and from the right background to connect and sympathise with Tess's lot and understand her worries and fears as she grows up in the novel. I could also, hopefully, learn from her mistakes and those of her friends and admirers.

Thomas Hardy writes sublimely about country matters and his novels are packed with social history and detail - I could, and still can, identify with so much of what Tess goes through in the novel as well as relishing the vivid and detailed description of life's trials and tribulations, and the highs and lows of communal work, a century and more ago.

# ALAN DAVIES
## *ACTOR*

My favourite book is **A PRAYER FOR OWEN MEANY** by John Irving.

# RICHARD DAWKINS

*PROFESSOR OF THE PUBLIC UNDERSTANDING OF SCIENCE AT OXFORD UNIVERSITY*

**THE LION CHILDREN** by Angus, Maisie and Travers McNeice is an astonishing book, by an even more astonishing trio of children. It's hard to describe: you have to read it, and once you start reading it you can't stop. Think of Arthur Ransome's **SWALLOWS AND AMAZONS**, except that this story is true and it all happens far from the comfort of England. Think of C S Lewis's **THE LION, THE WITCH AND THE WARDROBE**, except that the lion children need no magic wardrobe to pass through; no fake world of wonder. The real Africa, humanity's cradle, is more magical than anything C S Lewis could dream up. And, while they have no witch, these young authors do have a most remarkable mother ...

# ALAIN DE BOTTON
## *WRITER/PHILOSOPHER*

My favourite book is Cyril Connolly's **THE UNQUIET GRAVE.** The accusation most often levelled at this great book is that it is a work of pure egoism - an accusation that fails to distinguish between talking a lot about yourself (which can be very entertaining) and being self-centred (which never is). Connolly did a lot of the former, but was not the latter.

The book is a seductive mixture of diary, commonplace book, essay, travelogue and memoir - arranged in loose paragraphs in which Connolly gives us his views on women, religion, death, seduction, infatuation and literature.

The thoughts are wise, dark and beautifully modelled, with the balance of the best French aphorisms. For example: "There is no fury like an ex-wife searching for a new lover", "No-one over thirty-five is worth meeting who has not something to teach us - something more than we could learn from ourselves, from a book." The charm of the book lies in the narrator's mischievous, melancholy tone as he shifts between the sublime and the banal: "To sit late in a restaurant (especially when one has to pay the bill) is particularly conducive to angst, which does not affect us after snacks taken in an armchair with a book. Angst is an awareness of the waste of our time and ability, such as may be witnessed among people kept waiting by a hairdresser."

**THE UNQUIET GRAVE** is a book about a thousand

things, held together by the intelligence, candour and humour of the author. I'd find it hard to pursue a friendship with anyone who didn't have any sympathy for it - and hard to hate someone who did.

# DAME JUDI DENCH
## *ACTRESS*

My favourite book is **THE MAGUS** by John Fowles, closely followed by **DANIEL MARTIN** by the same author. I think John Fowles has to be my favourite author, although I find it disastrous to read any of his books - once I pick one up, I cannot put it down, so everything else gets ignored!

# COLIN DEXTER
## *WRITER*

Whilst working early in my career for Oxford University Examination Board, I was a member of a committee composed of dons and senior A-level English Literature examiners. At one point we were discussing passages, from one of the set texts, for inclusion in an examination paper. When, in my ignorance, I ventured my own opinions on the matter, the Chairman quietly but pointedly asked if I had ever read it. I confessed the truth, whereupon one of my colleagues gently suggested that the book should (surely!) be prominently displayed on the shelves of every educated person in the land; and others endorsed this view with such conviction, such sensitivity, that I could scarcely wait to rush out of the meeting to the nearest bookshop and buy it.

That book was Dickens' **BLEAK HOUSE** - a book that over these many years now I have come to regard as the greatest novel ever written in the English language.

# PETER DUNCAN
## *ACTOR/PRESENTER*

My favourite books at the moment are Philip Pullman's trilogy **NORTHERN LIGHTS, THE AMBER SPYGLASS** and **THE SUBTLE KNIFE.**

As well as being great adventure stories they incorporate three of my interests - William Blake, I Ching (the Chinese book of changes oracle) and dead gods! For my children, they are the greatest classics of their age.

# IAIN DUNCAN SMITH
## *POLITICIAN*

For my favourite book I have chosen Jane Austen's **PRIDE AND PREJUDICE** because it is a book one can read and re-read and always learn something about life and people whilst being entertained.

# NOEL EDMONDS

## *TV PRESENTER*

It's not easy choosing just one book even though I have to admit I'm more of a magazine reader than a bookworm.

I think the book that has most affected me in recent years is Tony Parsons' **MAN AND BOY**. He very carefully manipulates the reader, taking one from uncontrollable laughter to a serious lump in the throat page by page.

I'm also a huge fan of Jeremy Clarkson so I love the irreverence of **BORN TO BE RILED**. However, there are two other books that have most certainly proved invaluable recently. I live in a house with a wife and four daughters so you will appreciate that I am very much in the minority. Indeed, a friend of mine rather uncharitably says that I live in the Hormone Hotel! So, I really enjoyed reading **WHY MEN DON'T LISTEN AND WOMEN CAN'T READ MAPS** and also John Gray's **MEN ARE FROM MARS, WOMEN ARE FROM VENUS.**

If I had to nominate a favourite book of all time, it would probably be Kenneth Grahame's **THE WIND IN THE WILLOWS** simply because it brings back very happy memories of my childhood.

# HUW EDWARDS
## *NEWSCASTER*

**LUCKY JIM** by Kingsley Amis is simply a great read. Amis describes the life of a young college lecturer who finds himself in a dull, provincial town - and his exploits are recounted to hilarious effect. The characters, including puffed-up Professor Welch, and his prattish son, are comic classics. The scene where Ji m has to deliver a lecture, slightly the worse for wear, is one of the funniest in modern fiction. It is a biting satire on the small-minded obsessions of provincial academic life, but it's not done in a nasty way. It's just very, very funny. **LUCKY JIM** is rightly one of the classics, and no one who reads it comes away disappointed.

# BEN ELTON
## *COMEDIAN, PLAYWRIGHT AND DIRECTOR*

**ANIMAL FARM** by George Orwell is one of my favourite books, perhaps because it works as both a children's and an adult's book. I first encountered it when my mother read it to us when I was seven or eight. At the time I thought it a riveting and very moving personal tale about life on a farm run by animals. I can still remember crying at the part where Boxer the cart horse is carried away. As an adult I of course came to realise that the book is also an astute lesson in the history of a large part of the twentieth century and a brilliant critique on the politics of totalitarianism. Orwell is for me one of the great writers of the last century but if you want a laugh, turn to the equally different but rather different work of P G Wodehouse.

# SIR ALEX FERGUSON OBE
## *FOOTBALL MANAGER*

My favourite book when I was at school was Robert Louis Stevenson's **TREASURE ISLAND**. I enjoyed it because, as a young boy growing up by the docks in Glasgow seeing the large ships, I used to think about the book **TREASURE ISLAND,** which was a wonderful story.

# SIR RANULPH FIENNES
## *EXPLORER*

**GHORMENGHAST** by Mervyn Peake.

A wonderful story, a saga of somewhere strange that beats Tolkien into a cocked hat. Superb language and extraordinary imagination.

# ANTHONY FLEW
## *EMERITUS PROFESSOR, READING UNIVERSITY*

My chosen subject is Thomas Hobbes, author of a classic political philosophy entitled **LEVIATHAN**.

# PHILIPPA FORRESTER
## *TV PRESENTER*

I love books full stop. However, I have always particularly loved books by Gerald Durrell, and a favourite would have to be **MY FAMILY AND OTHER ANIMALS**. I love his passion, enthusiasm and humour.

# EDWARD FOX

## *ACTOR*

My favourite novel is called **DECLINE AND FALL**. Its author is Eveyln Waugh.

# GRAHAM GOOCH
## *CRICKET COACH*

My favourite book is **BOBBY MOORE'S AUTOBIOGRAPHY,** because as a young boy, growing up in London's East End, Bobby Moore was my hero and I was an avid West Ham United supporter.

# ROBERT GODDARD
## *WRITER*

I would put forward as my favourite book **THE MAGUS** by Joh n Fowles, because it is satisfying and intriguing on so many levels and is the novel I most often return to.

# CAROLINE GOODALL
## *ACTRESS*

When I was ten years old, I was given a magnificent copy of the **GREEK MYTHS AND LEGENDS**. I was transported by the travels of Odysseus, the squabbles of the Olympian gods and the mysteries of the Minotaur of Crete.

From this book grew my fascination for ancient civilisations. Today I have a home in Tuscany, close to the ancient capital of the Etruscans. The town is still encircled by 3,000-year-old walls.

An understanding of the past helps to put our present into perspective, a useful tool for these uncertain times.

My children now also love reading about the Greek myths. In fact all our animals are named after the Greek gods!

# MICHAEL GRADE
## *EXECUTIVE CHAIRMAN OF ITV*

My favourite book (at the moment) is **WAR DIARIES of FIELD MARSHALL ALAN BROOKE**. It is a day by day account of the man charged by Churchill to be effectively Chief Executive of World War Two. What ever doubts he had about the outcome of the war, he could only share with his diary. Churchill undoubtedly provided the political and inspirational leadership, but Alan Brooke's skills and character ensured that victory was delivered. What a man.

# SARAH GREENE
## *PRESENTER/ACTRESS*

One of my favourite books is **THE LION, THE WITCH AND THE WARDROBE** by C S Lewis. I first read it when I was eight, adapted and directed it as a piece of musical theatre at university, and hence have just read it to one of my god-daughters. It is magical, funny, sad, challenging and ultimately about what is good. It is also timeless.

# BARONESS SUSAN GREENFIELD

*PROFESSOR OF PHARMACOLOGY,*
*UNIVERSITY OF OXFORD*

My favourite book is **THE LEOPARD** by Guiseppe Tomasi Di Lampedusa and the reason why I like this so much is because it deals with issues that transcend cultures and eras around the theme that 'things have to change in order that they stay the same'.

# DR JOHN GRIBBIN
## *AUTHOR*

My favourite book changes from time to time, but I'll give you a go at a present one. The best book I've read is **DARWIN'S ORIGIN OF SPECIES**, which combines science, adventure and a kind of detective story, as well as being beautifully written. My favourite book (this week, at least!) is John Irving's **THE CIDER HOUSE RULES**. I'd hate to analyse the reason too deeply, in case I spoil the sheer pleasure of re-reading it from time to time, but the characters come across as real people and Irving creates a real sense of place and time, a time which (for all its faults) seems less frenetic and more desirable than the time we live in. Of course, that's illusion – but illusion is what I want from a novel.

# SOPHIE GRIGSON
## *FOOD WRITER/BROADCASTER*

I don't have one favourite book above all others, but one that I have adored since I was a teenager, and have read several times over the years, is **LE GRAND MEAULNES** (sometimes translated as The Lost Domain) by Alain Fournier. It begins in a schoolroom somewhere in the depths of the late nineteenth century (I think) Sologne, an area of France full of lakes and mists. Gradually it reveals a story of impossibly romantic, youthful love. The narrator tells the tale of his hero, Le Grand Meaulnes, finding quite by accident, a mysterious fairytale castle that appears to be ruled by children. Here Meaulnes falls in love with a beautiful young woman, but commits himself to a quest that will ultimately take him away from her.

The book is beautifully written, evoking the melancholy landscape of the area as it portrays a small group of adolescents as they enter adulthood. Like a Greek tragedy, you know that in the end all cannot be well. It makes me weep every time I read it. Marvellous stuff.

# DAVID HAFFNER FRGS
## *LANDSCAPE PAINTER/FORMER EXPLORER*
## *AND MOUNTAINEER*

Over forty years ago, high in the Norwegian arctic fjells of Vesteralen, I was given a copy of Henry David Thoreau's **WALDEN** to read whilst my elderly host made supper on our little hut stove.

It was October, frosty and clear. Outside, the night sky was like a watercolour palette where the greens, whites and pinks of the aurora mingled and ran together.

This was indeed the perfect setting for an introduction to Thoreau's unique writings and, as the fragrant aroma drifted up from the cooking pots, his ideals of living a simplified lifestyle and reaching for the "finer fruits of life" drifted through my receptive mind.

I read on long into the night and found spellbinding the extraordinary story of a failed schoolmaster and his experiment with living a self-sufficient life in the woods of New England more than a century ago.

Humankind is, I feel, adrift on very treacherous waters in the 21st century - perhaps the timeless message of **WALDEN** might still have some resonance for us today?

I hope that many more may find pleasure and inspiration in the words written so long ago on the shore of Walden Pond.

# SUSAN HAMPSHIRE
## *ACTRESS*

I have never been a great reader but, when it was part of work, I have always enjoyed reading, especially novels for the television series I have done. John Galsworthy's **THE FORSYTE SAGA**, W. Makepeace Thackeray's **VANITY FAIR** and also many of Anthony Trollope's novels as I did **THE PALLISERS** and also **BARCHESTER TOWERS**. So for a 'non-reader' I've had the joy of reading many good books. However, the strange thing is, the ones I've enjoyed most are books that were not for my work, namely, Laurie Lee's **CIDER WITH ROSIE** and Dostoevsky's **CRIME AND PUNISHMENT**, neither of which I did as television serials! There you go - there's nowt as strange as folk!

# JEREMY HARDY
## *WRITER/BROADCASTER/COMEDIAN*

My favourite book is **BORSTAL BOY** by Brendan Behan because of its enormous heart. It appears to be a ruthlessly honest account of Behan's time in Borstal, but he is not in the least judgemental, and although he is at times boastful he seems to be bragging on behalf of the human spirit, not just himself.

# SIR JOHN HARVEY-JONES
## *CORPORATE ADVISER*

My favourite book still has to be **THE WIND IN THE WILLOWS**. It showed an ability to draw characters and characteristics, which I have observed during almost all of my working and business life. Moreover, it was and still is a 'rattling' good read, and one couldn't ask for much more of any book.

# NIGEL HAVERS
## *ACTOR*

My own personal favourite book is **NOSTROMO** by Joseph Conrad. I first read this book at school and it has continued to fascinate me through many readings. As well as the main plot, which centres round a tin mine in South America during the Victorian era, this story takes in all of life's complexities such as relationships, religion, ethics and politics. Each time I read it I discover something new and surprising.

# STEPHEN HENDRY
## *PROFESSIONAL SNOOKER PLAYER*

My favourite book is **KITCHEN CONFIDENTIAL** by Anthony Bourdian. I found the book very interesting in how he started his career and ended up being a celebrity chef.

# IAN HISLOP
### *BROADCASTER/EDITOR OF 'PRIVATE EYE'*

My favourite book is **ENGLAND, THEIR ENGLAND** by A MacDonnell.

# GLENN HODDLE

## *FOOTBALL MANAGER*

My favourite books are **WHITE EAGLE** (Books 1, 2 and 3).

# GEOFFREY HOWE
# OF ABERAVON, CH, QC
## *HOUSE OF LORDS*

For my favourite book, I am happy to propose **MORNING** by Julian Fane, published by John Murray in 1956 and now in its eighth edition.

I was lucky enough to read it when first published and ever since it has remained the one book that I have no hesitation in recommending to everyone! It is a beautifully written, immensely perceptive tale of childhood and of the impact upon the young personality of a host of childhood experiences. Affectionate, perceptive and deeply moving - and ready to be re-read as often as you might like.

**MORNING** was hailed by Lord David Cecil as "a remarkable, fresh, strong, beautiful book" and described by Harold Nicholson as "the work of a literary artist, beautifully written, coloured and composed". Sir John Betjeman said that it seemed to him "to deserve to last for generations" and Elizabeth Bowen that "it has what no-one should miss - real distinction and unusual beauty".

Julian Fane is still writing - his most recent publication **DAMNATION** led a reviewer in *The Tablet* to describe him as a "writer so good one wonders why he is not better known than he is". I absolutely share that view - and hope that my choice of **MORNING** for your own charity book will promote his cause as much as yours.

# JOHN INVERDALE
## *SPORTS PRESENTER*

A book I would wholeheartedly recommend is Lance Armstrong's **IT'S NOT ABOUT THE BIKE**: you don't have to be a cycling fan to enjoy it - it's just a wonderful tale about the human spirit and personal fulfilment.

# LOUISE JAMESON
*ACTRESS*

My favourite book? Such a hard question. It has to be the works of Shakespeare but, for a good read, any Bernice Reubens book. My latest lovely read was **THE DIVINE SECRETS OF THE YA YA SISTERHOOD** by Rebecca Wells.

# BORIS JOHNSON
## *MAYOR OF LONDON*

My favourite book is **THE ILIAD** because it tells you all you need to know about life, death and the vital necessity of failure.

# CHRIS KELLY
## *PRESENTER/WRITER/PRODUCER*

I think my favourite book is a novel by the great American writer, Carson McCullers. It was her first, published when she was only twenty-three.

**THE HEART IS A LONELY HUNTER** (wonderful title) is an extraordinary portrait of small-town life in the Deep South. The characters McCullers creates are strange and unforgettable - the deaf-mute, mysterious guardian of the town's secrets; the young girl, Mick, who can't wait to grow up; Jake, tense with unbearable rage ... McCullers' insights into the mind of the adult male, or female come to that, have never been bettered by man or woman, and yet here she was, not long out of her teens.

Her writing is unlike anyone else's. She draws you into the heat of that town in the very first sentence: "In the town there were two mutes, and they were always together ..." and she never lets go.

Doubtless the fragile state of her own health contributed to her understanding of loneliness and the search for love. After a series of strokes she was paralysed down her left side at the age of thirty-one. But that didn't stop her making a unique contribution to the riddles of the human heart.

# MARTIN KEMP
## *ACTOR*

My favourite book is **TRAVEL** by Michael Crichton, which I found great to read and an inspirational book.

# CHARLES KENNEDY
## *POLITICIAN*

My favourite book is **THE DAY OF THE JACKAL** by Frederick Forsyth. I believe it is a classic contribution to the thriller genre. It is a gripping story about a man who is known only as The Jackal, the worl d's most dangerous but elusive assassin.

The story follows the path of Forsyth's two central characters: The Jackal and the man employed to track him down. The Jackal is hired by a rebellious organisation to murder the French President, Charles de Gaulle. And so, The Jackal prepares for his most important moment; his final and most challenging murder. The man sent after him is only a simple inspector in the French police, with no information and little time. As the minutes count down to the final act of execution, it seems to the reader that there is no power on earth that can stop The Jackal.

# SIR LUDOVIC KENNEDY
## *WRITER/BROADCASTER*

As a child I adored the Winnie-the-Pooh Books and his friends Piglet, Owl, Eeyore - and of course Christopher Robin who I played cricket against when his prep school took on mine. I also came to enjoy the satirical verses written about him, viz.,

*Hush, hush, whisper who dares?*
*Christopher Robin has fallen downstairs.*

Grown up, my favourite became **THE AGE OF REASON** by Thomas Paine, first published in Paris at the end of the eighteenth century. The reason I like it so much is that it demolishes many of the myths of Christianity.

# NIGEL KENNEDY
## *VIOLINIST*


My favourite book is **THE UNCONSOLED** by Ken Ishiguro because "it's really good" and I have never been disappointed with any of his books.

# GLENYS KINNOCK
## *MEMBER OF THE EUROPEAN PARLIAMENT*

Jane Austen, the Brontës, Dickens - where do you begin to identify a favourite book? There is no replacement for losing yourself in a book and, for me, reading a novel is the very best form of relaxation - you could even say that a good book keeps me sane!

In the summer of 2003 I read **THE GREAT GATSBY**, so I have decided to choose this modern classic, which is such a brilliant story of post-war America, as my current favourite. Gatsby is a tragic figure whose dreams and aspirations tell us so much about that time when there was such a preoccupation with style, wealth and status. It is a beautifully crafted story, which is on a par with many other great novels - there is poetry in the writing and there is enchantment, suspense and mystery, and an enormous sadness. I love it.

# The Late DAVID KOSSOFF
*AUTHOR/ILLUSTRATOR*

One of my favourite books is one of my own. It was written in 1971 to follow the big success of my **BIBLE STORIES RETOLD** (1968), which was Old Testament. **THE BOOK OF WITNESSES**, my New Testament book is truthfully one of my favourite books. In 'shape' it is the taken-down statements of forty 'witnesses' who must have been around during the life of Jesus. Each is described, and speaks. When you've read the book you have read the whole thing: from the Annunciation (to Mary's aunt Elizabeth) to the empty tomb.

I made them up, but the book is honest. "If it bothers you, good reader", it says, "that the witnesses are fictional, comfort yourself that what they tell of is true. It is gospel."

It is my bedside book. It is a dip-in book. It reminds me of how I could once write, for now I am old and too lazy for such things. In truth I do not read many books. I sculpt and paint and doze after lunch. The book, by the way, has never been out of print.

# OLIVER LETWIN
## *POLITICIAN*

My favourite book is **PORTRAIT OF A LADY** by Henry James, which was the first great novel that I ever read. I recall opening it when I was 16, in the expectation of spending a few months reading the first few pages, as part of an A-level English course, and discovering many hours later, to my astonishment, that I had been unable to put it down.

The power of James' characterisations, and the bizarre twists of the dense plot, lead me back to the book every few years - and I carry around with me always the aroma of the settings by the Thames in England, and in Rome.

# GARY LINEKER
## *SPORTS PRESENTER*

I always find it very difficult to choose one book! However, when I was young my favourite books were the **FAMOUS FIVE** stories by Enid Blyton. As a child, I loved the crisp writing style, the sense of adventure in the stories and that the Five always seemed to be eating! Re-reading the books now with my own two boys I am fascinated by their view of the writing style and the way the books immediately transport me back to my own childhood.

# KEN LOACH
## *FILM AND TELEVISION DIRECTOR*

Page for page, probably the most important book I have read is **THE ENGLISH REVOLUTION 1940** by Christopher Hill, an Oxford historian. It is short, not much more than an essay, but in its brief pages you can read the real significance of the civil war that saw Charles I executed and a republican government under Cromwell.

One conventional view has been that parliament stood for the rights of the people against a king who wished to rule with absolute power, who would raise taxes without parliament's consent and act in an arbitrary and absolutist way.  A contrary opinion, the high Tory position, has been that Charles spoke 'not for my own right alone, as I am your King, but for the true liberty of all my subjects', that his execution was a crime and that his opponents were self-serving men doomed to failure.  Both views come together in seeing the subsequent re-establishment of the monarchy and the settlement that followed later as the basis for our great democracy.

Hill turns this judgement on its head.  He shows that the civil war was a class war, in which 'the despotism of Charles I was defended by the reactionary forces of the established church and conservative landlords'. Against this, Parliament stood for the interests not of the common people but of the merchants and traders, rich farmers and gentry.  The struggle against the old order attracted many who wanted to establish a new order of society altogether; the Levellers, Diggers and other groups whose words have rung down the centuries: 'Property divides the whole world into parties and is cause of all wars and bloodshed and contention everywhere'.

Why does this matter to us now? Well, we live with its consequences. In the intervening centuries we have gained the apparatus for democracy but not the substance. Power still lies with big business, the international corporations, the oligarchs and the politicians who act on their behalf. The class that took power in seventeenth century England retains it to this day. The myth that the changes made then were on behalf of 'the people' is very convenient for our present leaders.

Christopher Hill's brilliant little book shows that if we want a true democracy we need another social change. To complete the above quotation: 'When the earth becomes a common treasury again, as it must ... then this enmity in all lands will cease'.

# RAY LONNEN
## *ACTOR*

My favourite book is **THE DIARY OF A NOBODY** by George and Weedon Grossmith. I love the humour it contains - the pomposity and self-importance of Pooter, the main character, who, after all, is only a humble clerk in a run-of-the-mill office. He keeps a diary of the events in his day-to-day life as if they were of immense significance. Great pride and pomposity are constantly pricked, but he never seems to know about it.

# JOHN McARDLE
## *ACTOR*

There are many books I have read that have moved and entertained me, but no more so than Sebastian Faulkes' **BIRDSONG**. This book follows a young officer from before the Great War, during and after. It is a love story and a war story. It carries all human emotions - love, grief, despair, anger, and man's inhumanity to man. It makes you think about all those young men cut down at the start of their lives. It is a book you cannot put down once started.

# JULIA McKENZIE
## *ACTRESS/DIRECTOR*

How can you ever say what makes one book your all-time favourite? Certainly, I have read **ACT ONE** by Moss Hart many times and always find something fresh and incisive. Of course, it is a sort of bible for the stage, and so obviously my 'inner man' responds to it time and time again. I chose it for the book on 'Desert Island Discs' many years ago and I haven't changed my mind.

# SALLY MAGNUSSON
## *PRESENTER*

My favourite book is **KIDNAPPED** by Robert Louis Stevenson.

I love Stevenson's writing and this is a wonderful evocation of Scotland in the years following the Jacobite rebellion.

# JOHN MAJOR, CH
## *FORMER PRIME MINISTER*

One favourite book that springs immediately to mind is **FAME IS THE SPUR** by Howard Spring. A wonderful novel that depicts the birth of the Labour Party and of the rise of a fictional young Member of Parliament whose life - at least in parts - appears to be based on Ramsay MacDonald. The fictional character begins life in the poorest of circumstances with great principles, and sheds both principles and friends as he moves towards the upper echelons of political life. It is full of insights that are as relevant today as they were when the book was written over half a century ago.

# PATRICK MALAHIDE
## *ACTOR*

Along my bookshelves, ranged in good naval order, is a line of books by Patrick O'Brian. They are known to their avid readers worldwide as the Aubrey/Maturin novels, and they deal with every nook and cranny of shipboard life under the White Ensign at the time of Nelson. It would be invidious to single out a particular volume, as the twenty books were conceived as a unified whole, a great sweep of history under sail - bloody, passionate and, above all, bristling with detail, detail, detail ...

# PETER MANDELSON
## *BUSINESS MINISTER*

My favourite book is **GRAPES OF WRATH** by John Steinbeck. The struggle of the Joad family's journey from America's dustbowl to the promised land of California during the Depression is a timeless classic. Telling of the difficulties, tragedies and injustices that visit them on their journey, it is also a powerful tale of the strength of the human spirit.

Against dire poverty and people exploiting their desperation, the characters of Tom, looking to go straight after prison and Ma, who struggles to keep the family together against the odds, are great figures. The stunning ending offers a message of hope for the family and their fellow migrants, and concludes a powerful story that has inspired my belief in social justice and the importance of working together to make things better.

# BILL MAYNARD
## *ACTOR*

The book that has had the most profound effect on my life is **THE POWER OF POSITIVE THI NKING** by Norman Vincent Peale.

# BEL MOONEY
## *WRITER*

I first read **MIDDLEMARCH** when I was in the sixth form at Trowbridge Girls' High School. My wonderful English master, Denis Boulding advised me to give it a try, (in his laconic, imaginative way of thrusting me further and further towards great books) and his word was law. I had read **SILAS MARNER** and **THE MILL ON THE FLOSS** but my teacher told me that to read **MIDDLEMARCH** was a different order of experience and that he felt me 'mature' enough. The lure of flattery as easily as powerful as that of literature, and so I began.

I can still remember the heady, addictive fall into George Eliot's provincial world, the greedy reading in the solitude of my bedroom, the desperation that Dorothea should not marry Casaubon nor Lydgate be trapped by the poisonous Rosamund Vincy. Still I can revisit, in imagination, the powerful emotions aroused by my first reading of George Eliot's sublime closing paragraphs. They never fail to move me to tears, and I do not believe there are finer words in the whole of our literature.

**MIDDLEMARCH** spoke to me of the vast dignity and potential of what is ordinary, and of the imaginative sympathy will all living things which are part of the redemptive function of art. Its sweep was equal to that of Doctor Zhivago, even without the framework of great political and historical events. I read with awe George Eliot's account of how the vainglorious Mrs Bulstrode finds humility and love in forgiving her husband the disgrace he has brought upon them: '...now that punishment had befallen him it was not possible for her in any sense to forsake him'.

Was any other writer capable of such knowledge and such compassion? At seventeen I doubted it – and still feel the same. I once heard Martin Amis dismissing the morality of George Eliot, maintaining she tells people what not to do. What arrant nonsense! She says, 'This, right and wrong, is what people DO, how they are, and willy nilly, it is all capable of being understood.

I have re-read **MIDDLEMARCH** four or five times, and writing this, itch to revisit its world again soon. It hardly seems possible, but each time I find the novel even greater, discovering things in it as if for the first time. Like a religious fanatic I would convert all people to my faith; read **MIDDLEMARCH** and hold a glass to your own soul, in its infinite possibility of greatness.

# DESMOND MORRIS
## *WRITER*

My favourite book is **A VIEW OF THE PEOPLE OF THE WHOLE WORLD** by John Bulwer (1654).

This was the first illustrated book to bring together examples of the strange customs to be found all over the world. Bulwer was a London doctor in the reign of Charles I, and he was fascinated by the ways in which different tribes displayed their bodies. His wonderful illustrations show people with peculiar fashions in elongated ears, filed teeth, stretched lips, pierced noses, and so on, taking each bit of the body in turn and examining the many ways in which people have enlarged, tattooed, decorated and modified them.

Although he was clearly intrigued by the ways in which different cultures had such different ideas of beauty, and showed his readers for the first time the amazing variety of human body-fashions that existed around the globe, he was at pains to voice his strong disapproval. In his opinion, the human body should be left alone and not tampered with for the sake of local fashion. He referred to exotic fashions from faraway places as: "The mad and cruell gallantry, foolish bravery, ridiculous beauty, filthy fineness and loathsome loveliness of most nations, fashioning and altering their bodies from the mould intended by nature." But this did not stop him making a thorough examination of every extreme fashion he could uncover.

This is a favourite book of mine because it is a pioneering work. In a sense, it is the first true anthropology, the first attempt to show the extraordinary cultural variety of our species.

To buy a copy today would cost several thousand pounds, but it is my hope that, one day, a new edition of it will appear to show modern readers how the fascination with cultural diversity - which we take for granted today - first began, back in the 17th century.

# SAM NEILL

## *ACTOR*

My favourite book is really two books, but may be read as one - **GORMENGHAST** and **TITUS GROAN** by Mervyn Peake.

Peake was an extraordinary and unique talent, a very particular voice. In these books he creates a marvellously graphic imaginary world full of vivid characters; heroes, villains, the beautiful and the grotesque. Like all the best books they take you somewhere you've never been before, and cannot be put aside. And after you've finished them they never leave you.

# BILL ODDIE
## *WRITER/ACTOR/BROADCASTER*

I find it extremely difficult to select just one book as a favourite, but I'm certainly a fan of Kenneth Grahame's **THE WIND IN THE WILLOWS.**

# DAVID OWEN CH
## *HOUSE OF LORDS*

It is always very hard to single out one book, but I think I would choose **SNOW GOOSE** by Paul Gallico, illustrated by Peter Scott. It is a hauntingly beautiful story of the relationship between a young girl, a disabled man and a goose and a little sailing boat, rescuing men off the beaches of Dunkirk.

# NICHOLAS OWEN
## *NEWSCASTER*

My favourite book is Charles Dickens' **NICHOLAS NICKELBY.** It plunges from extreme gloom, with the cruelties of a Yorkshire school based on one in an area I know well, to great heights of joy and happiness. All human life is there, and I have loved the work since I first read it in my early teens.

# GEOFFREY PALMER

## *ACTOR*

One of my favourite books is **THE SHIPPING NEWS** by E. Annie Proulx.

# JEREMY PAXMAN
*JOURNALIST/AUTHOR/BROADCASTER*

I don't really have a single favourite book. How do you choose between, say, Tolstoy's **WAR AND PEACE** and Garcia Marquez's **ONE HUNDRED YEARS OF SOLITUDE?**

# BILL PERTWEE
### *ACTOR/COMEDIAN*

My first memory of my favourite book was my mother reading to me a few pages every night as a bedtime story. I suppose I must have been about five. She had no trouble in getting me to go to bed on subsequent nights as I was always anxious to know what was going to happen next to my four friends; Mole, Ratty, Toad and Mr Badger.

Yes, you've guessed it! Kenneth Grahame's **THE WIND IN THE WILLOWS** (illustrated by E H Shepard). Later, as I was able to read it myself, it was a book I turned to many times - perhaps just reading the odd chapter, or my favourite bits. I still do that to this day.

Those wonderful characters, with their human-like qualities, hopes and fears.

Mole, so house-proud, but yearning for a life beyond his little home, so one day he puts down his paintbrush and goes off in search of adventure, thinking to himself that there must be more to life than whitewashing his house.

Ratty, the cheerful optimist, who loves the riverbank and all it means to him. Expressing the view (held by many I'm glad to say) that there simply isn't anything more wonderful than messing about in boats.
Dear old Toad, so full of himself, with always a new-fangled idea or hobby, and never taking advice until too late, when disaster strikes. Filled with remorse for at least five minutes and then he's off again on some mad-

brained scheme.

The wise old Mr Badger, who lives in the Wild Wood, so sensible, so right, always with the solution to the problems, proclaiming "The time has come!"

Then the wonderful climax when the weasels and stoats are vanquished and all is well again.

Every story should have a happy ending, that's what stories are for. I believe that books are making a great come back at the moment and that is a wonderful thing. All children should be encouraged to read, to enter that marvellous world of make-believe.

My wife, Marion, remembers never being bored as a child, as long as she had a book and an apple! Her favourites were the Swallows and Amazon books by Arthur Ransome, with **COOT CLUB** taking first prize. That's all about sailing on the Norfolk Broads, "messing about in boats" in fact. So you see, we do have something in common!

# TIM PIGOTT-SMITH
## *ACTOR*

I honestly don't have an all-time favourite book; as people, we change, and, as we change, the books we like tend to alter. I didn't like Evelyn Waugh's **BRIDESHEAD REVISITED** the first time I read it, nor the second; the third time, I thought it was a work of genius! Clearly it was I who had changed, and not the book!

The book I am going to commend is not therefore my all-time favourite! However, it is a book that I really enjoy, and one that I recommend to people who say they are fed up with reading, or don't like reading. I gave it to one adult friend who said he had never finished a book; he couldn't put it down! It is an inexplicably little-known work, by the inexplicably little-known contemporary American writer, Thomas Eidsen. I discovered him in the mid-nineties, and have now read all his books - there are only four that I know of! This one is called **ST AGNES' STAND:** it is, at root, a western. Although that may explain why the book has not been given the profile it deserves, don't let the fact that it is a western put you off. This is a western with a difference.

Set over a hundred years ago, it is the story of an escaping convict who encounters a group of nuns that has been ambushed by the Apache. That summary doesn't do the book any favours either! However, it is not the narrative in itself that makes the book such a great read, it is the internal journey of the convict and his conscience that is so compelling; the fact that it is a great story makes it, in addition, a real page-turner. Eidsen also writes with a powerful, poetic simplicity that is a real pleasure to read. The only warning I would post is that it may be a bit more of a boy's book than a girl's.

Making recommendations to people is always tricky. There are several other books that I really love, but I am certain that this one will be enjoyed - devoured! - by anyone who bothers to pick it up and start turning the pages.

# JONATHAN PRYCE
## *ACTOR*

My favourite book is usually the last book I've read; in this case **PNIN** by Nabokov. It is beautifully written in the kind of English that is often only used when it is someone's second language - the kind that has you reaching for the dictionary every few chapters. It paints wonderful pictures of its characters, especially Pnin himself, but essentially it is a book about novel-writing itself. It is witty and highly intelligent; everything I want to be when I grow up!

# PETER PURVES
## *PRESENTER/WRITER/PRODUCER/ DIRECTOR/ACTOR*

My favourite book? What an impossible question to answer. Every book I read has its place - it may fit the mood I am in, or my state of health, or my desire for information or escapism. And at different times of my life (i.e. different ages) books have different degrees of importance.

Currently Terry Pratchett is one of those writers I never tire of. His Discworld novels are always enjoyable, sometimes black, and sometimes very light. They are always funny and sometimes disturbing. Always an excellent read, and pretty hard to classify.

On the same level, one of the most enjoyable books I have ever read was in a similar vein - T H White's **THE ONCE AND FUTURE KING**. It is the story of King Arthur from childhood to death. Book 1 is very funny and childlike. A wonderful fantasy about questing Knights and Arthur (Wart) growing up as a page and later a Knight himself. Then it becomes a very dark book indeed, and gives much cause for thought.

In my early thirties I really enjoyed Robert Shea's **THE ILLUMINATUS TRILOGY**. It has been recently re-published, but when I tried to read it again last year, I found it totally unreadable tosh.

Arthur Heller's World War Two epic satire **CATCH 22** must come into the reckoning somewhere. I tried to read it twice, the first time getting no further than page 22, and the second time stopping at page 15. Then, on holiday a year later, I picked it up and devoured the entire thing in two days. Fabulous book.

I love the old Myths and Legends, so Homer's **ILIAD** and **ODYSSEY** are amongst my favourite books. Not, I hasten to add, in the original Greek, but in the Penguin modern translations. What a magnificent storyteller he was, old Homer. And in spite of the many repetitions, both books hold the attention throughout.

I read three or four books a month - I thoroughly enjoy good espionage, and intrigue. I most recently have enjoyed Martin Cruz Smith's **TOKYO STATION**, and have always enjoyed his books from **GORKY PARK** onwards.

But none of this is getting me any nearer to choosing my favourite book of all time. At times I have enjoyed Samuel Butler - **EREWHON** was a fine read. But I suppose if you judge a book by the number of times you read it, then **GULLIVER'S TRAVELS** by Jonathan Swift must rate very high indeed. I have read it four times in all, and, of course, it is a series of books, not just about a Giant in Lilliput, but a number of serious satires on the mores of the time, with his various journeys to extraordinary places; Brobdingnag, with its magnificent sophisticated horses, being my most favourite section.

I currently also enjoy Gerald Seymour, Tom Clancy and Michael Crichton's books. And I drop into quite a number of non-fiction works.

# IAN RANKIN
## *WRITER*

I don't know if it's my favourite book or not, but the novel that has had the biggest effect on my life is probably **A CLOCKWORK ORANGE** by Anthony Burgess. I don't know if it's true or not, but I remember hearing a story that Burgess wrote several novels in a very short space of time, having learned (as he thought) that he didn't have long to live. These books were written to support his family after his death. Well, he didn't die, but he did produce the amazing dystopia of **A CLOCKWORK ORANGE.**

Why was the book so important to me? Well, I grew up in what some would have said was a fairly dispiriting place: a coal-mining village in the 1960s/1970s ... only the coal had run out, and a lot of hope and vitality seemed to have disappeared with it. My home town was a rough, tough place, and I felt a bit lost. I was in my early teens, and spent a lot of time in my bedroom, listening to Pink Floyd and writing song lyrics which I never showed to anyone. I knew that if any of my peers knew what I was up to, they'd laugh at me or, worse still, would give me a good kicking. But I was fairly good at seeming to fit in. I would hang around the local high street with my peers, while they spat at passing cars and drew up plans for pitched battles with gangs from neighbouring towns. I was careful always to remain on the periphery: watching, studying, memorising.

This was not a literate community. My parents didn't read many books. There was no bookshop in the town, only a small library funded by the miners. I haunted that place, and did the same thing with the library at my high school. My peers passed round pulp fiction paperbacks, books with titles like 'Skinhead' and 'Suedehead'. These were often badly-written and exploitative.

But then something happened. A pal handed me his big brother's battered copy of a book that had first been published in the early '60s. It was **A CLOCKWORK ORANGE**. I knew of the film. It had come and gone, having been withdrawn from circulation by director Stanley Kubrick after incidents of copycat violence. I'd never managed to see it. But I devoured the book. Here was someone writing about my community, about the frustrations and fears of teenage males, about their aggressive tendencies and confusion about their place in the world. But Burgess was writing very literate prose. This was one of my first encounters with actual 'literature'. I re-read the book, then re-read it again. I probably read it six or seven times that first year. (I've still got my pal's brother's copy: somehow it never found its way back to him.) Then I went one stage further: I started to mimic the book's style, producing stories and anecdotes about my own town, my own life. I started to become a writer.

None of those early attempts ever made it into print, but I came to love writing. It was my way of dealing with the world around me, or creating order from the chaos of the everyday. I could examine myself and explain myself. I could produce whole universes from the tight confines of my bedroom. I could grow and travel beyond the village that had been my home. I could taste new freedoms.

The best books still give me that shiver down the spine,

that sense of being offered glimpses of new possibilities. I became a writer, thanks to Anthony Burgess's **A CLOCKWORK ORANGE.**

# CLAIRE RAYNER
## *WRITER*

I'm happy to tell you what my favourite book is - it's called **THE GOOD COMPANIONS** by J B Priestley. It was the first adult book I read as a child and it has never lost its value for me. It's a superb picaresque novel that displays pre-war England in all its glory; its seediness and its misery as well as its fun. I love every word of it and re-read it frequently.

# WILLIAM ROACH MBE
## ACTOR

My favourite book is one of esoteric teachings of philosophy from other realms called **THE PHILOSOPHY OF SILVER BIRCH** (editor Stella Storm).

It explains what we are and describes how we should live our lives. If everyone were to follow its teachings all the problems of the world would be solved in an instant.

It is a book to keep by the bed and to dip into from time to time rather than just read straight through, as there is much to think about.

# TONY ROBINSON
## *PRESENTER/JOURNALIST/WRITER*

I love George Eliot, Dickens, C S Forrester and Stendhal. To tell you the truth I'd read anything on anyone's bookshelf with the possible exception of Jeffrey Archer. But the best new novel I've read in the last couple of years is Barbara Kingsolver's **THE POISONWOOD BIBLE**. I won't spoil it for you by giving the plot away, but please read it.

# ANDREW SACHS
## *ACTOR/WRITER/NARRATOR*

Note: Andrew wrote this preface to **MY FAMILY AND OTHER ANIMALS** by Gerald Durrell several years ago.

There are many books on my shelves that have been with me since childhood. I still get pleasure from re-reading them, or at least from turning my head to one side and scanning their spines. Many of the pages are brown around the edges, crumbling away, and independent enough to flutter off at the first sign of a breeze. No longer can I lose myself in these relics from youth while tramping through the streets head down and bruising the occasional lamp-post. They are now strictly for indoor use only. Which is more sensible anyway, and certainly less painful.

One of these treasures is a frail paperback copy of **MY FAMILY AND OTHER ANIMALS**. On the cover are some rather good thumbnail sketches of our thirteen-year-old Gerry on his stomach, feet in the air, elbows spiked to the ground in support of the head as he studies the vegetation before him. A smiling dog - Roger of course - sits at his side. They are surrounded by other members of the cast: an owl, a tortoise, a gecko eyeing up a praying mantis, several other relatives (human), and even a penguin in its own oval frame - though curiously enough there is no mention of it in the story itself.

I was a slow reader. A book of 300 pages was a daunting

prospect, and only my passion for wildlife allowed me to carry on, and then only by ruthlessly skipping over any deviations from the main theme.

At the time I read it I was about the same age as Gerry - or so I thought; but studying the cover again, I noticed a strange anomaly - the price was 3s 6d. that's 17.5p in today's money, and more than I could have afforded at thirteen. In those days a shilling (5p) was my top price for a paperback. What was wrong? I checked inside for the date of my edition: 1962. Well, no wonder. Thirteen? Rubbish. I was closer to thirty! It was the magical storytelling itself that had turned the clock back for me.

Now, another forty years later and older, and with happy visits to the Jersey zoo that bears his name, I'm into the book again, and you know what? I'm back to being thirteen, with the added pleasure of enjoying the more grown-up bits as well now.

And never mind only reading indoors. Corfu under cover? Never. That's for sissies. This morning I sauntered blissfully through my neighbourhood on foot ... and buckled a tree. But who cares? It's nice to realise that one's special boyhood heroes need never die. For me they are, among others, Stanley and Livingstone, Charles Darwin, Lassie, Edgar Rice Burroughs, Johnny Weissmuller, Burton and Speke ... and Gerald Durrell.

# PAMELA SALEM
## *ACTRESS*


My favourite book - this is hard! I love different books for different reasons. However, **TALES FROM THE ARABIAN NIGHTS** filled my head with stories that stimulated my imagination and expanded my mind with unusual and vivid scenes.

And, of course - A A Milne's **WINNIE THE POOH**.

# PRUNELLA SCALES
## *ACTRESS/DIRECTOR*

My favourite books are **THROUGH THE LOOKING GLASS** by Lewis Carroll and **ROGET'S THESAURUS OF ENGLISH WORDS AND PHRASES.**

# WILL SELF
## *WRITER*

In answer to your question, I cannot say that I necessarily have a favourite book. However, there are two books that have been key influences in my own development as a writer. One of them is **ALICE'S ADVENTURES IN WONDERLAND** by Lewis Carroll and the other is **CATCH 22** by Joseph Heller. **ALICE IN WONDERLAND** was a book I was exposed to at such a young age that it became part of the structure of imaginative categories within which I view the world. Its strange and sly blend of humour and surrealism has infiltrated my perception of what it is for a work to constitute fiction.

Joseph Heller's **CATCH 22** is a kind of manual of satire, offering all the different techniques that are essential for a satirist, from comic exaggeration to wilful obfuscation to farce to parody and so forth.

These two books, between them, had a profound influence on me.

# DR JOHN SENTAMU
## *THE ARCHBISHOP OF YORK*

My favourite book is **THE HOLY BIBLE** as it has inspired my life.

# JOHN SESSIONS
## *ACTOR*

**A PORTRAIT OF THE ARTIST AS A YOUNG MAN**
by James Joyce. An appreciation by John Sessions.

I was lucky enough to have this book as one of my A-level set texts. I've read hundreds of novels since and I've yet to read a book more perfectly conceived and executed. On the face of it, the story is quite simple. We have a brilliant, difficult Dublin boy - Joyce's alter ego - battling with his Jesuit upbringing as he forges his own individual identity as an artist. Joyce's style, though, is wholly revolutionary. Thought association is just one of the devices he uses to create the boy's completely authentic psyche. It is a profoundly emotional book while never falling prey to boneless sentimentality. It might be a bit priggish to say that it's a David Copperfield for grown-ups, but it's hard to shy away from there being an element of truth to such an assertion (I nearly chose **DAVID COPPERFIELD** as it happens, so I don't know where that leaves me!) Like David Copperfield (which it's really nothing like), it contains scenes you remember all your life, particularly the row over Parnell at Christmas dinner and the sermon on eternal damnation. Joyce, the artist, involves us totally in Stephen Dedalus's story, while retaining a ruthless objectivity as he fashions his art. He is 'A God paring his finger nails', to use his memorable phrase from the novel.

# CAROL SMILLIE
## *TV PRESENTER*

Favourite adult book: **I DON'T KNOW HOW SHE DOES IT** by Alison Pearson.

Favourite kid's book: **CLARICE BEAN, THAT'S ME** by Lauren Child.

# ALISON STEADMAN
*ACTRESS*

When I finish a good book, I always feel a sense of loss, and I'm slightly depressed, but then I discover another and that day is fine.

Ian McEwan is one of my favourite novelists. **A CHILD IN TIME** is a wonderful book. It's quite frightening and takes you on a long and strange journey. I found myself crying reading it on the tube. Such was its impact. I hope you find the joy of reading too.

# MICHAELA STRACHAN
## *PRESENTER*

In answer to your question, my favourite book as a child was **BORN FREE**. It gave me a love of wildlife and Africa where I now spend a lot of my time. I used to fantasise about being Joy Adamson and looking after orphaned lions. By presenting wildlife programmes such as 'The Really Wild Show' I guess I've almost achieved that fantasy. I have obviously read many good books since - but it remains one of my favourites.

# EDWARD STOURTON
## *NEWSCASTER*

Looking along my groaning shelves I find it very difficult to choose a favourite title, but I would settle on Tolstoy's **ANNA KARENINA**. Of course, the heroine's adulterous passion and suicide are the driving narrative force behind the book, but for me it is the wonderfully rich account of the relationship between Kitty and Levin that raises it to greatness - in fact I sometimes suspect the Anna story is there simply as a foil to bring the much more complex picture of their marriage into sharper relief. Levin must have been enraging to live with at times - as was Tolstoy himself - and one or two of his displays of emotional maladroitness would be difficult to match. But he is a fundamentally good man, and Tolstoy manages the rare trick of giving us a character who is both a hero and a human being. He can write instinctively from within the minds of women and children as well as those of men, so **ANNA KARENINA** is peopled with a cast who stay with you as friends and foes long after you have closed the last page. And the plots and sub-plots are handled with a skill that must surely make any soap scriptwriter green with envy.

# UNA STUBBS
## *ACTRESS*

My favourite book is **CRIME AND PUNISHMENT** by Dostoevsky because I found it the greatest thriller ever. I was pushed to read it and put it off because I thought it would be difficult, and was surprised to find it easy and so gripping.

# DAVID SUCHET OBE
## *ACTOR*

My favourite book is **MASTER AND COMMANDER** by Patrick O'Brian. I was introduced to this author only a short while ago and from page one I entered the world of the British navy in the 19th century.

The characterisations are truly full of very interesting dimensions and his descriptions of what it must have been like on board the ships are second to none.

I was so taken with this first of 18 stories that centre around the two leading characters of Aubrey and Maturin, that I have just bought the second called **POST CAPTAIN**. I can't wait to start it. Patrick O'Brian has to rank as a really first-class writer. I have never enjoyed a novel about the sea more.

# MOLLIE SUGDEN
## *ACTRESS*

What a difficult question! There are so many books that I have enjoyed. Perhaps I had better say **THE WIND IN THE WILLOWS** by Kenneth Grahame, since that was the first 'full length' book that I read as a child, and it encouraged me to continue reading, thus giving me pleasure for a lifetime.

# CHRIS TARRANT
## *RADIO AND TV PRESENTER*

I have always read avidly since I was quite a young boy and now my own son, Toby, is also a very keen reader. I like to see it - I think it's very healthy; too many kids spend too much time staring mindlessly at TV screens these days and I think reading is altogether better for them.

I seem to remember lots of Enid Blyton books when I was very young and then it was all the R L Stevenson stuff, **TREASURE ISLAND**, etc. For some reason I always hated anything with Paddington Bear, Rupert Bear or Pooh Bear in - which is very strange because I absolutely love bears and have spent hundreds of hours watching them in the wild in Canada and Alaska!

As a teenager, I became very keen on Thomas Hardy books, the Brontë sisters' **WUTHERING HEIGHTS**, and **JANE EYRE** and even Dostoevsky!

As a student, things were rather different as I took a degree in English Literature so I was obliged to read all sorts of books. I suppose it was essential at the time but it did mean that I overdosed on the works of people like Charles Dickens, Jane Austen and Mark Twain and I've never really been able to read them again.

I still read whenever I can, although it tends to be mainly on aeroplanes and holidays. In recent years, since we bought a house near Cannes, I've been reading a lot of French history.

The book that stands out in my mind the most - and I read it before I'd ever heard of the film - was **SILENCE OF THE LAMBS** by Thomas Harris. It absolutely frightened the life out of me but I was gripped and couldn't put it down for two days! And I'm currently right in the middle of the latest book by Frederick Forsyth.

I've also read just about every fishing book ever written!!

# NORMAN TEBBIT CH
## *HOUSE OF LORDS*

I am not sure that I have a lasting favourite book. The book I turn to most often is Dr Hessayon's **GARDEN TROUBLES EXPERT** but I would not call it my favourite.

At the moment I am reading Orwell's **1984** so it has become my current favourite, but I very often take down my Penguin **POEMS OF THE GREAT WAR** to read just one poem to put my life back into perspective, so perhaps that is another favourite.

# GEOFF THOMPSON
## *AUTHOR*

My favourite book is **WATERSHIP DOWN** by Richard Adams. When I read this book I was a young man that desperately wanted to become a writer (my outrageous vision). I was in a safe warren (my marriage, my job, my life) but I innately knew that if I didn't vacate soon, disaster would sweep through my world. Looking back **WATERSHIP DOWN** inspired my first step away from the known and the ordinary and the speciously safe. And one step led to two steps and two steps led to three, and before I knew it I was running, and searching and (yes my friends) buccaneering. Many of my old (rabbit) friends did not take the journey with me of course, and that made the move all the scarier. But, I figured that scary was where it was at, it spelled the end of mediocrity and spawned the beginning of new adventure.

If you follow adventure you are bound to find your own watership down. I hope you do. I did.

# BILL TIDY

## *CARTOONIST*

# ALAN TITCHMARSH MBE
## *BROADCASTER/WRITER*

My favourite book is **BLANDINGS CASTLE** by P. G. Wodehouse, because the weather's always sunny, and it makes me laugh out loud.

# RICKY TOMLINSON
## *ACTOR/WRITER*

The best book I have ever read is **THE RAGGED TROUSERED PHILANTHROPISTS** by Robert Tressell.

# JAYNE TORVILL OBE
## *FORMER WORLD CHAMPION FIGURE SKATER*

One of my favourite books would have to be **ANGELA'S ASHES** by Frank McCourt.

# ANTHEA TURNER
## *TV PERSONALITY*

My favourite book of all time is **THE LION, THE WITCH AND THE WARDROBE** by C S Lewis. This children's story is beautifully written, can also be enjoyed by adult readers and carries a message that none of us can ignore.

# DR CHAD VARAH,
# CH, CBE, MA (Oxon)
### *FOUNDER OF THE 'SAMARITANS'*

I have many favourite books and James Branch Cabell's **JURGEN** is hard to obtain. The latest I read all through at a sitting was Sandor Marai's **EMBERS**, published by Penguin, translated beautifully from the Hungarian. The one before that was Margaret Atwood's **ORYX AND CRAKE**, a believable and horrifying picture of the world a thousand years hence.

# JEREMY VINE
## *TV/RADIO PRESENTER*

The book I've most enjoyed reading recently is **THE CORRECTIONS** by Jonathan Franzen. It's about the devastation that Parkinson's disease can cause in a family, and I loved it because it drew me closer and closer with some wonderfully touching detail. It's an amazing novel.

# CAROL VORDERMAN MBE
## *TV PRESENTER*

When I was aged between 10 and 13, I wasn't interested in science fiction, but later on amongst my favourite 'reads' were:

**THE HITCHHIKER'S GUIDE TO THE GALAXY** by Douglas Adams; and **SURELY YOU'RE JOKING, MR FEYNMAN!** by Richard P Feynman.

Richard Feynman won the Nobel Prize in 1965 and was one of the world's greatest theoretical physicists. He had a mischievous quality about him and a tremendous zest for life which was contagious. His conversations with his friend Ralph Leighton were taped and form the book. They are very funny and not at all dull. They are super stories as well as being informative. The *Good Book Guide* said that Richard Feynman is the kind of physicist you'd expect to meet in the pages of a Douglas Adams book - only he was real.

# ZOË WANAMAKER CBE
## *ACTRESS*

I would like to nominate **MRS JORDAN'S PROFESSION** by Claire Tomalin because Ms Tomalin brilliantly animates her lead character, the actress Dora Jordan, the 13 Jordan children, her weak royal partner (later King William IV) and the theatre itself. It is meticulous biography at its creative best.

# PAULINE WEBB
## *PREACHER AND BROADCASTER*

You asked me to name my favourite book, which is very difficult to do, but I think my favourite, which I frequently turn to, is a book of sermons by Martin Luther King, entitled **STRENGTH TO LOVE.** I love this because the sermons in it are not only excellent expositions of difficult Bible texts but also are a kind of manifesto underlying the whole of Martin Luther King's ministry, which became a modern martyrdom. I was privileged to be in New York at the time when he was leading his Civil Rights campaign and counted it a privilege to march along behind him. I count him as among God's great prophets, whose words we still need to hear today.

# DENISE WELCH
### *ACTRESS*

I have never been a great reader of books, especially since becoming an adult when work and family seem to take up so much of my time, except on holidays when I do like to get into a potboiler sometimes.

I think of all the books I have read, however, **LITTLE WOMEN** by Louisa May Alcott has left the greatest impression. I am not sure I can say why at any length except that it was very evocative of my childhood which was very happy for me.

We lived on the coast in the North East. I have a younger sister and we had a very stable upbringing. I enjoyed school, had lots of friends and enjoyed family holidays, mostly in this country. I never felt any of the pressures that children seem to have these days and I certainly was not a natural scholar! I found **LITTLE WOMEN** a comfortable read.

# COLIN WELLAND
## *ACTOR/WRITER*

My favourite book remains **WUTHERING HEIGHTS** by Emily Brontë. A powerful 'one-off' in which an entrapped genius releases all her frustrations in a powerful melodrama brilliantly written and set in the wilds of unfashionable Victorian Yorkshire. A gem!

# JUNE WHITFIELD CBE
## *ACTRESS*

A book I enjoyed very much was **CHOCOLAT** by Joanne Harris. I am not a 'chocoholic' but after reading the book which - apart from being a good story - conjured up visions and aromas of chocolate delicacies, it was a near thing.

**CHOCOLAT** is a feast and a very good read.

# ANN WIDDECOMBE
## *POLITICIAN*

My favourite book is **THE WIND IN THE WILLOWS** by Kenneth Grahame. This charming tale of the riverbank is much more than just a children's story. All my life I have been meeting gentle, unworldly Moles, energetic Ratties, wise Badgers, rebellious Weasels and pompous Toads.

# ROWAN WILLIAMS
## *ARCHBISHOP OF CANTERBURY*

**THE MAN ON A DONKEY** by Hilda Prescott.

**THE MAN ON A DONKEY** is an historical novel which focuses particularly on events in the traumatic 1530s leading up to the Pilgrimage of Grace. It is one of my favourite books because of the way it shows the mysterious nature of how people decide and change in times of crisis, and also how God works in completely unexpected ways. And the book does all this in a way that makes you care deeply about the people in the story.

# RICHARD WILSON
## *ACTOR/DIRECTOR*

Michael Faber's **THE CRIMSON PETAL AND T HE WHITE** is a book that has been a great pleasure to me in recent months. It is a big, sprawling novel set in London of the 1870s and the author's grasp of historical detail and minutiae is quite extraordinary.

Although I am always a bit daunted when I see a big thick book, I can assure people who make the effort that it is well worth it. Faber has a very original style of writing and the pages turn almost automatically. It is a book you don't like putting down and the character of 'Sugar' will surely be remembered by those who meet her in many years to come. Read it and enjoy.

# TERRY WOGAN OBE
## *TV AND RADIO PRESENTER/WRITER*

Reading and books are one of life's greatest pleasures. It's impossible to give one favourite book - there are so many.

These days, I rarely stick with a book that is boring me, no matter what its reputation or recommendation.

I always have a P G Wodehouse by me and something by William Trevor.

One of my favourites is **MISS SMILLA'S FEELING FOR SNOW** by Peter Hoeg which gives an extraordinary insight into the workings of a Greenlander's mind. And **BIRDSONG** by Sebastian Faulkes is one of the greatest novels of the past 20 years. If you haven't already read it - I dare you to put it down.

# ANTONY WORRALL THOMPSON MOGB
## *TV CHEF*

My favourite book is **A PASSAGE TO INDIA** by E M Forster. My grandfather lived in India for 38 years and my mother was born in India so there is a strong link to that country. Whenever I go back to reading this book it's like retracing my grandfather's footsteps.

www.apexpublishing.co.uk